Doll Apollo

Doll Apollo

poems

MELISSA
GINSBURG

Louisiana State University Press   *Baton Rouge*

Published by Louisiana State University Press
lsupress.org

LSU Press Paperback Original

DESIGNER: Michelle A. Neustrom
TYPEFACE: Adobe Garamond Pro

COVER IMAGES: Astronaut and toile courtesy Shutterstock. Cream background texture courtesy Unsplash/Annie Spratt.

LIBRARY OF CONGRESS CATALOGING-IN-PUBLICATION DATA
Names: Ginsburg, Melissa, author.
Title: Doll Apollo : poems / Melissa Ginsburg.
Description: Baton Rouge : Louisiana State University Press, [2022]
Identifiers: LCCN 2022023256 (print) | LCCN 2022023257 (ebook) | ISBN 978-0-8071-7739-6 (paperback) | ISBN 978-0-8071-7827-0 (epub) | ISBN 978-0-8071-7828-7 (pdf)
Subjects: LCGFT: Poetry.
Classification: LCC PS3607.I4587 D65 2022 (print) | LCC PS3607.I4587 (ebook) | DDC 811/.6—dc23/eng/20220518
LC record available at https://lccn.loc.gov/2022023256
LC ebook record available at https://lccn.loc.gov/2022023257

My mind leads me to speak now of forms changed
into new bodies

—OVID's *Metamorphoses,*
trans. Charles Martin

Contents

Daphne / 1

Doll

Paper Girls / 5

Craft Day / 6

Genealogy of the Garland / 7

Miss Paper / 8

She's an Animal in the Sack / 9

Song of the Shred / 10

In the Paper Dollhouse All the Rooms
    Collapse / 11

In an Endless Chevron Landscape a
    Cutout Doll and a Stick Figure
    Meet but Cannot Touch / 12

Chevron / 13

Framed / 14

One Cannot Read Oneself without
    Great Difficulty / 15

Integrity of the Fragment / 16

Paper Dreams / 17

The First Fold She Ever Learned / 18

The Shreds Speak a Language Too
    Connected to the Past / 19

Paper Trail / 20

Apollo

The Faked Apollo Moon
    Landing / 23

Apollo / 25

Apologia / 26

Apollo the Vessel Sheds His
    Parts / 27

Speaking as the Moon / 28

What's the Moon / 29

My Body like a Diner Fills with
    Astronauts / 30

Apollo Sleeps and Dreams of
    Transport / 31

[Neil Armstrong] / 32

Apollo Imagines the Edge of
    a Field / 34

When Doubt Comes to Apollo / 35

The Moon Now / 36

Apollo in Orbit Remembers the
    Earth / 37

For Those Who Doubt, for Those
    Who Believe / 38

Toile

How the Plateau Formed / 41

Toile de Jouy / 42

Pastoral / 46

There Comes a Summer / 48

History / 49

To the Meadow a House Is
    a Rupture / 50

Under the Fields / 51

The Origin of Trees / 52

The Bench / 54

Tigers / 55

Weren't We Here Before, When It
    Was Warm / 57

Séance / 58

Toil / 59

The Adder / 60

Night / 62

Sky / 63

Whitetail in the Rain Moving
    About / 64

Acknowledgments / 65

Doll Apollo

Daphne

halted mid stride
un-nymphed as mayflies
laureled & wreathed

newly rooting   yet

      even as a girl she had that mentholated
      breath   loved bay loved

      riverbank   played house
      for hawks

      had that crown in her
           that stillness

when asked
      does she   miss the chase

at each petiole
unrolls a glossy nib

     a bit of shade   a blade
to lean against the flesh

to leaf the grove is no arrest

Doll

Paper Girls

The women slosh
the girls in vats the women spin
the fibers. The women dry

and press the sheets.
The women stack the women
and gather them in reams.

The women do this work
to their past selves
they are happy to bleach

clean, pulp, and soak
in a vat. Slurry stings
the skin, an act

of preparation.
It separates the girls
from the women.

The women are hunters
after a fashion.
They hunt

themselves and fashion
the tools
they are made of.

Craft Day

Scissors cut
through the snowflaked

morning. Dolly
sharpens her edges.

Trims herself, gives herself
fringe. Makes more like her.

Sisters, clones. She scissors
their slick

magazines, girlskins
sleek as blades.

She hones her scissors
On sandpaper. She will marry

that abrasion. Make it
scrape her. She'll

feel it. She'll unfold
garlands.

Genealogy of the Garland

Template mother,

original doll,

façade wrinkled all the way through,

receipt shoved in a pocket.

With hands like hinges, turn the page

as though you are not the page.

You are a door opening,

not a folded note. Not

a pamphlet. Not a map.

Bark from a tree

on the land the map lies for.

Life force, sap rising.

The tree shoves buds into flower

like tufts of paper.

Miss Paper

she is thin
and white her
torn bits ruffle

she transcribed she
blown about has
caught ink she

blacks out
erasures
thin her further

she traces
after masters
poorly prints her

secret names she
leaves crumpled an
old coupon a

two-for-one
she makes a
dress a cat

of herself she
wears herself thin
she pets it

She's an Animal in the Sack

Dolly sees herself   in the pond's
flat plane.   She lines
the bank

with the cattails,
bending to touch
      their own necks.

Wind disrupts the surface, upsets
      her angles, dogears her corners.

Pleats and tucks, makes her a crane.

Origami Dolly, animal

    in the sack, bucking
    against rough burlap.

Burlesque of the pond's edge,
weighted choreograph. String
      tied at the top.

She soaks and sinks.
    Sheds pulp in mud

below a willow's   continual fall, continual
rise to the surface.

Snakes swim under. Lay
their nest of eggs. Heat-sensing
      pits in their faces.

Song of the Shred

The ink bled through and I easy tore.
How it goes,
Your ugliest mistake was done, you to yourself,
Your weakness on display
Rends the heart of the stain.

In the Paper Dollhouse All the Rooms Collapse

The cutout girl looks out the punched-out
window, thinks   of perforation
and the rectangle   she came from,
the self-shaped hole she filed away.

And what is the self   wearing
        her drawn-on   undergarments,
        curling edges   in danger of tearing,
            the self   is never naked,

the self   may be pressed
between heavy books.

In the heavy books, the old saying:
        If you try to make paper dolls do anything at all
        their clothes fall off, they can't stand up,
        the tabs slip the slots.

A house made of dolls is a delicate system.
Architecture of held breath.

Say the window is a body
like yourself   that you look into
and out of.

                           All flat planes
the self perceives   as bodies

like the self. The self can be leafed.
Every book is a prison of sisters.

In an Endless Chevron Landscape a Cutout Doll and a Stick Figure Meet but Cannot Touch

On red and white chevron
pattern unending

        a doll

awaits severance.
She valleys.

        She repeats
        in regular intervals

her decorous patience.

        A figure is given
        lines like picks and ropes.

Made mountaineer
to climb a red slope.

        The climber's
        thin collection

of angles moves across her

        potential dollscape.
        Latency crimped.

Chevron

This world—   dye &

       valley valley valley

    No selvedge edge

         No fray   No cliff

               No table's edge
               below which   scraps

without edge or end   without variation   & yet—

    Wrinkle in the fabric. Crisscross
        of threads
    independent of the stripe.

    The weave has its own order
        the dye
    does not penetrate.

    At a precise point in the depth
        of the weave, V's
    cease. The weave reticulates.

Framed

The doll felt framed.
Her alibi failed, she felt

arrested. She felt jail.
She could've slipped through

the bars at any moment
but didn't—

They threatened
confetti.

This doll is like an old jail
kids learn about in school.

This doll is a field trip
no one has fun on.

There aren't enough
lunches. The sun

is cold. The girls fall
into a huddle and mutter

      Cold doll jail doll old doll
      Felt doll wool doll school doll
      Field doll fun doll trick doll
      Moll doll will call doll
      Hotel doll call girl doll

They whisper, She's just paper,
they mat her.

One Cannot Read Oneself without Great Difficulty

And then I became a folded note

To become a note   is to become a vehicle

which drives to the time   of waiting to be read
and parks there   wanting it:

        to carry import
        to drink the oils
        from sets of fingers

But it was no fault of mine I was a note

the words rode   on top of my self
and were not me   in that parking lot

        that pile of sealed envelopes

I spent
much energy trying   to shake the marks

        dear   *I'm*   *sorry*

        I wish we'd   *never*

I waited   quaking under ink

wanting the fingers and the eraser   the eyes
of the circulars   variously glossed

Integrity of the Fragment

Still am an arm.

Miss not my sisters.

Holding posies wrapped in a blue bow,
My five individual fingers.

Miss not my body
Of sisters.
                    Scraps wheeling past
                                        In the wind.

I am slender, deckled.

                                I have these flowers.

Paper Dreams

Rag paper dreams rag dreams,
Newsprint dreams of the wood chipper,

Doll paper dreams tabs-in-slots,
Dreams the sheet

From which
She was punched.

How close it felt to free,
Uniting all those tiny holes

To outline
Her in air.

Dream paper dreams dream dreams,
Forest floor,

How clean it was, the forest
Of chainsaws, how renewable.

The First Fold She Ever Learned

She accordion-held
               her sisters' hands.
Garland
               of reverb
purple and dusty
               as the old
mimeograph.
               The mapping fold,
the joining
               of fingerless
palms
               at the crease.
Thigh on
               thigh, symmetry
redoubling
               each rib and clavicle
to its equal
               on the next
girl in line.
               That kinship.
What we were all
               cut out for.
To be splayed
               over the entry.

The Shreds Speak a Language Too Connected to the Past

was shoulder

was

garment

was passion

was

arms

the kind with metal brackets

at the joints

was

in a heap
on the floor

among many other papers

was   covered in

script was

erased

encountered   storm

was

uncared for   was

knee

was freckled   taped back

and again

rent

Paper Trail

Dolly finally slips from the folder,
as she was always bound to
                   at a fountain

in the center of the square, traffic coursing
through the roundabout. She shouldn't

be there, should be buried in a book,
she's been told to keep away

from wet. The spray takes no time
         to dissolve her tender skin,

return her to that pulp of youth—
                         days as debris
                         in the bottom of the barrel.
                         Fibers loosening her aspen.

When she was a tree she drew water from the soil
through xylem vessels.

She formed the cells and felt
them die, leaving hard cell walls stacking
root to leaf.

Felt water travel
and evaporate through her leaves and hover

in a cloud
above each green page,
those humid individual weathers.

Apollo

A doubt is an idea that is still alive.
—MISHKAN T'FILAH

The Faked Apollo Moon Landing

a parabolic arc of dust
behind the rover's wheels

binds me to you
                    Earth

the way you make things heavy
blow air into a space

already filled with air
            the way you hide

your stars in the sky you flag
                        waving army

you scientists
                with your answers

at the edge of the crater
            starless black

multiple light
                sources multiple

shadows   the doubts
                        creep in

the sky behind me creep
            outside   the viewfinder

the doubts lap basalt waves

bring your war out from its shadows

show it the stars
show it the moon

Apollo

Wolf god. Sheep god. God trapped in a mine. God of fields and flowers. Of pastures and herds. God of exoskeletons. Hunter and flayer, feeder of snakes. Healer god of arrows, of oracles you will never figure out. God of colonies and the crying rock. Unshorn god. Shining god of mice and islands.

Wolf of healing. God in the womb already frightening. Killer of cyclops maker of lightning. God of moderation. Monster of light. Tender protector. Hunter god liar god. Colonizing god, god of ships leaving, of sun in the sky, of tunnels and holes, of sowing a seed. Slayer of Python. God of the deal.

Farm god. Lover god. God of my sister Artemis goddess of that sleek lens through which I look, the moon. God of ships and a sun. Supplier god, contract god. Twin god and wave god. Waving goodbye on the dock and the ship leaving god on a wave.

God of the oracle stops. God of compromise and centuries. God of whispered riddles swallowed on an island. Snake-eaten god. God of dried up waters, cratering depths. Canyon, erosion, billowing out. Tributary god cut off from its source. God of the dry bed, of the cold war. Together with Artemis slayer of progeny. Husband the silvered arrows. Quiver in the outskirts of the sky.

Apologia

Apollo, I'm no better
astronaut than sailor's

knot. No better leash
than a sailor. I'm a sailor's

if he'll have me. I'm a house
keeper, not a good one,

my house a carapace. An
elegant brooch punctuates

my collar. My sailor's suit-
or, I'm a cupful of medicine

I swallow like a tongue
hides to spit and bury—not

till you stop watching.
I'm patient. I'm punctured.

I'm going soon. Perhaps I'll be
grateful, perhaps from space

for your boats full
of goods pointed at me.

Apollo the Vessel
Sheds His Parts

my Saturn my thrust
my fuelspent shell
twirls off Canaveral

abandoned fawn
turning circles
in a barn something
neurological wrong

its eyes closed the right half
of its body stuck praying
to a three-cornered god
the left in wet hay

mewling some nerve
damage something
pressing on the spine

goodbye what got me out
rust in oceanspace
mollusk open let the
eels glide through

Speaking as the Moon

I bare my curve
to the missing air

to thinness
to distance

to fractions   shadow   night

lonely as a female
dark

      you made
a revolution
a measurable
arc

for which   you lay
your light   you stole
your light   you gave away

What's the Moon

just a phase   a sliver
whittled   & hung

       full   circle
       feet   sunk

in fire-smelling   dust

My Body like a Diner Fills with Astronauts

In footsteps in jetsam and titanium white I split apart I miss my thrust and light my kneeling piece my scientists litter oceans orbits televisions I will never leave this husbandry I am myself fallen in the ocean sunbleached Canaveraled washed in atmospheric gaps my windows vacant as the heads of astronauts my eyes like beakers of clear liquid measured in a vacuum on the empty sound stage there may I launch and launch may I blink and bend the lights

Apollo Sleeps and Dreams of Transport

In the dream a whippoorwill traveled by box. Four
roses aloof, the abyss leaning. Debris in every dock. Your
lame facsimile of spun silk pleasure, silver fox fur.
                    Eau de vie.
                    Bliss-plain sea-pill.

Suppose you spill forever.

Yew trained as a gallows tree. Kiln afever, smoking.

[Neil Armstrong]

Feel farm strong
like from driving fenceposts
like from trenching
to divert the sluice

☽

Steel charms long
for a clasp, pray in tethers
for the chain

☽

Mealworms elong-
ate under moonlight

☽

The alarm's on
trust me you want it
when I'm gone, you want precaution

☽

Keel harmed, long
gash on the hull of the craft

☽

Peal our song
toll clang howl
and knell

☽

Kneel, arms wrong
impossible to cross
the suit bulks and shines and mediates

☽

Steal far beyond
the dead volcanoes and lava flows
the tranquil sea
the marsh of sleep

☽

We'll mar dawn's
long shadows, put your

Teal garment on
let's walk around, make
this goddess a surface

Apollo Imagines the Edge of a Field

Pines lit with fireblight
Needles burn in absent

Blaze the pear's steep trunk
Shears and falls viburnum

Tracks a hawk
Blackberry roots

Travel the clay
A season of blossoms

Drops
  from every fruit

Sugars form the moon
Pales and waits

For me
  to shred the night

When Doubt Comes to Apollo

doubt arrives assured in her stumbling
doubt scatters at Apollo's feet
doubt falls about the god
in a cloud

                to trust
a thing such as a god
as much as the god trusts his own
appetite: doubt tries it but hesitates

in space the liquid doubt
does not pour freely but forms
a floating orb
              and dances slow before
the god's faces

doubt marries for love the altar of questions
      busies herself with the arrangements

                  doubt will not require
a television   to see the event
doubt   stitched in the shoes
          watches from the moment after the step

doubt has been married so long to the altar

each star a tribute doubt hunted and placed
                  on a plate

The Moon Now

We mined a sliver
to the craft

not stole, it was already mine
as my sister Artemis is

mine own slivered protocol
slender in

her protective suit
crafted and threaded

exquisite stitches
her arrow travels

yet untested
moondust clings to

new and full alike

Apollo in Orbit Remembers the Earth

the rocky shore

grows blue, moraine leans to the still river

    cirrocumulus chain a steep Brazil of phlox

        twill   torn

            unlocked and roaring
            hollyhocks, spores

blowing through the frame

For Those Who Doubt,
for Those Who Believe

O inconstant sound stage in the sky
O surface of shadows with one
frayed edge   receiver

of light and men above the field
owls hunt in the night and sound their calls

O broadcast O threat
        Let the field rats take cover

Let the voles and rabbits
breathe in the shadow
of the barn

Hunted at night and hiding
hearts beat in brambles
grown thick and safe

Blackberry fermenting on the vine
holds the smell of sun

O field light erode the bordering sky

Toile

How the Plateau Formed

Started dark and quiet
pool of field like the rest,
jagged grasses, land flat

as a tender sky.
Found in the sky a lofted model
and in its own grubby collections

of worms and roots
no recognition, no affection.
Waved seedheads, sought birds.

Wanted the sky's touch
and stretched. Sheared the faces.

Toile de Jouy

Was a background.
A weave in the toile.
Threads
Behind a village scene

Parasols, hunting
Party, hoopskirts.
Old oak. Picnic party.
Basketful

Of sandwiches
Spread quilt, a textile
Ground.
Printed on.

Unnoted, as music
Refuses to be written. To
Sound   stranded.
Drowned

In footsteps,
Horse sweat.
Pointers and setters
At the horses' feet, dust

Carried from their eyes
On tears. Made
Of holes, of air
Made thermal.

Made friction
essential. Fell out
Of a loom
As droplets

Separate from air
Find themselves
Heavy unable to
Stop

Pooling in a cup.
Was air once.
Now drown.
Was strands catching

Strands. Was
Run through.
Hemmed.
Inked

In a zoom out
A wave's retreat
Carries sand with it
Carries a picnic.

As a print color
Matches
Not quite up.
As a pinking

Cut prevents unraveling
Not completely.
As shears slipped
In a pocket a basket

Lined with fabric.
Ladies
In dresses ladies
In carriages.

Between the village
And the nap
Between dress
Pocket and the twisted

Fiber: dye
Commits, insinuates.
Woodcuts
Handprinted. Vats

Of color
Parsed. Was berries
Once was fruit
Of the black walnut

Shrubs of indigo
In a hot climate.
Between villages
Parties

Between parties
Bare nap
Sunbleached
Having been left

Between vignettes.
No road depicted.
World of arrival
But not travel.

Between threads
Ravaged
Fiber
Bit of silk

Caught
On brambles.
Beneath rifles
Shod hoof

Bit of grass
Between villages
Fibers
Between parties

Carnage
Between dye
And raw
Village

In the distance
Packs
Of wild
Dogs

Pastoral

I was unincorporated
I was without a body
I was lots
Not lots yet parcels

I was ground
Where the pipes will go
I was shrubs I was
Brush and the space

Between shacks I lacked
Governance I was
Lean-tos I was dens
In the earth and

Roots of the weak
Sweetgum I was pear
And turtle sunning
I was lungs un-

Breathing I was the site
On the horse's neck
Where bats came
Nightly to feed I was

The blood coagulating
Into morning I was
Waiting for full dark
Again I was waiting

For the wound
To reopen I was led
To a tree a weak
Tree strung with nets

I was the bat hoping
To be caught I
Couldn't heal myself
Fast enough

There Comes a Summer

the pond turns over
catfish fat as a thigh
float whitely trailing
their whiskers algae
blooms red under
the pollen film
fills a layer and climbs
fish confined above the harsh
sulfur and methane
of the thermocline
know aeration's poverty
by the heart thudding
in deep sediment brief
heavy thunderstorm
in summer is enough
to stratify and strip the water's
oxygen bring harsh gases
to the flush of sky
that grazes pond
and fishes' undersides

History

Volcano bled fire
and covered the moors.

Terrain like a sheet wrinkled.
In the desert an airplane dehisced.

Genes paired and shivered
in vain artifice.

Scree filled the bedrock floor.
Detritus, our ingenue.

The land was innocent.
War sizes ran small.

We kept the kills quiet
amid rows of pale clover,

sugarcane and millet.

To the Meadow a House Is a Rupture

Divided carpets stream

across each visible field

camouflage and horizontal slit.

fields the view overlooks.

close. Have a bullet.

beige problems

each hunting blind

Indoors afflicts

Deer keep the treeline

There's plenty of views.

Under the Fields

In the absence of desire
The objects of desire

Toil and weep

Perform our contrition
We tread like

Echoes
We are armies

Of apology

Carve into the earth
Tunnels   like foxes

Orange fur
In the stubbled field

Glows bright as an error

Tufts the warren
In darkness   our Lord
And our Container

The Origin of Trees

You believed
   that trees were geese who stayed
     and grew long legs.

   Believed a stream
     conveyed the sky from day
       to night, like a belt.

It's true the conveyer belt
   lies like a horizon, that rollers
     turn invisibly under land's last

     apparent point. The geese visit
       one pond then another, molt
         and eat the seeds we spread.

Down reels along the bank,
   a feather catches a poplar.
     Every tenth leaf turns

   its pale side
     to the sky. I like to lie
       and think of horizontals

from a prone position.
    As for belief,
    Have I conveyed my position?

   It is spatial,
     philosophical,
       semi-conscientious.

Prone to distance,
      lies and stars, myths
           frozen and flocked.

The Bench

for Chris Offutt

Between farms outside town

in a lot at the bottom of the woods

we parked. We walked up

crunching new snow.

A hill had been placed there.

Given no color, no depth. Only

white, etched in blue. Forms solid as farms

disappeared. We were figures

in a sketch of a cold deer path.

I did not expect to survive

such flattening. Then you said look

for a perfectly straight horizontal line

and under a mound of blue snow

such a line appeared.

Tigers

for Erik Lemke (1979–2012)

A hummingbird flies into a window
that looks like the sky. Everything around here

looks like the sky. The sky is tiger striped.
They call that kind of cloud

something. I know somebody
who knows about clouds. I could find

out. Everything around here
has a name.

☽

The hummingbird fell to the deck. My husband picked it up.

     —What did it feel like in your hand?
     —Nothing. It felt like nothing.
     —Where is it now?
     —Gone.
     —Dead?
     —Not dead. It flew away. It disappeared and it disappeared again.

☽

I'll tell you a joke. A hummingbird flew into a window.

I'll tell you another joke. Treachery,
we were friends once.

☽

In dreams the bird
weighs more, so you can feel it

when you pick it up. so when
it dies it seems

like something actually happened.
It's a sign bound around your hand

and a mylar star at the stripped road,
stuffed and shining.

Points radiate
from the helium center. The bird

weighs nothing waits nowhere.
The sky

looks like a window
and it flies right through.

Weren't We Here Before, When It Was Warm

weren't there tendrils   new shoots
didn't someone   shoot

it was deer season   the hay bale
     deep in the woods above the creek a target

rifles sounding from the fields out back
a spotted fawn   small as a cat

shot by children
    practicing   couldn't I have

    held it in my arms
wasn't there a new bow tied in double knots
that came undone

wasn't there a double bourbon
    and pushing the button   on the dishwasher
hundreds of times

when it was warm   wasn't the creek a path

    the hayfield inhaling gold breath
    vegetation blocked our sightlines

didn't the tall straight oak fall over the creek

and become   long
and become   a bridge

      a dead bridge   and bring
         the earth up with it

Séance

The buzzard's investigation

ripples   shadows

          across scrub,

sketching the roots

of a thermal. The usual

séance: hawks

on the ground,

          moss on

      a bent branch.

Icicles fall in the road,

just   ghosts

communicating. This message

has   no content no

      science no animals.

Toil

one must first make an incision in the fabric
in order to speak

fabric, from the workers
in metal and stone, later a building

or machine
something skillfully produced

artisans hewing their hard materials

an incision is hardly a made thing, more
an undoing
of thousands of intermingled fibers, a severance

as the pressing of flowers
is an undoing but also a preservation

one must first choose the specimen
free from rain or dew

one must split a thick blossom
in order to flatten

The Adder

May the pond be free
from its companion   pondwater
blackening   the pond's edges

      slipping   as it does
to the sides   behind
      below   a swimming   adder

May the air and the sky be excused
from one another   as a child
from a table   as a table

from its planes the   house from
its frame   Free
      garden from dirt

      garden
from sprouts waxing
white and long under layers

of mulch   Part spring from cold part
wood from grain part grain part monstrous
shout   Part splinter

from wood   splinter from flesh
Toss it in the fire
divorce fire

from its color its tremble and
its burn
      Divorce: does a door

need a wall to become itself
to separate
           from to open to allow

Night

The moonlight field manufactures night.
The factory workers take their smoke break

at the same time. They take time, stuff it
in their pipes,

puffing away, wasting it. It's never coming back.
The walls of the field are built of smoke. Workers

link segments of night in the moonlight,
connecting the tongue and groove.

A pond disrupts the field
like a smoke break a night shift: flicker

of light, moon leaning on the bank, small fire
doused in the flush surface.

As the makers of night make night,
as night is time and ends, this world drowns

its workers, the makers of the world.
Moonlight lightning fireflies fire

disappear forever. The workers
flash, swim, fit

the planks, sand them smooth,
sweep the field with the night.

Sky

to accommodate migration the sky

rips a series of bird-shaped

holes in its cloth

to accommodate the lawn it rips

its lower edge to fringe

the sky is a loose net

a thousand mouths

hinging at each wingbeat

its eyes like the gray inside a museum

the color of a docent's shadow on the wall

if the bird moves out of sync with the

sky's eyes blinking

one may enter the open shard

the brand new room of bird-filtered light

Whitetail in the Rain Moving About

to lure the deer install the salt

acquire the sack of corn and scatter

red clover

chicory orchard grass give them

fruit in the rainstorm give them

such a mineral they cannot turn from you

give them the pea plant the acorn

the encounter

the encounter you want

the meadow embouchure

paint the orchid scent on the bottoms

of your shoes and walk into the herd

shore of unshed velvet

Acknowledgments

Many of the poems in the "Apollo" section were published in 2021 as the limited-edition hand-printed chapbook *Apollo* with Condensery Press. Thank-you to Jan Verberkmoes and Andrew Dally for their beautiful work and support.

Some of these poems appeared in the chapbook *Double Blind* (Dancing Girl Press) as well as in the following journals: Academy of American Poets *Poem-a-Day, Bennington Review, Berkeley Poetry Review, Blackbird, The Boiler, Boulevard, Descant, DIAGRAM, Dream Pop Press, Guernica, The Kenyon Review, The New Yorker, Poetry Daily, The Rumpus, Southwest Review,* and *West Branch.*

Thank-you to friends and readers: Shane McCrae, January Gill O'Neil, Derrick Harriell, Kristi Maxwell, Kristina Marie Darling, Jeffrey Levine, Adrie Rose, Mary Romero Ferguson, Sarah Chestnut, Marc Rahe, and Chris Offutt, who walks this field with me.

Printed in the USA
CPSIA information can be obtained
at www.ICGtesting.com
LVHW092239230224
772664LV00003B/373

9 780807 177396